Charles
F. Lummis

Charles F. Lummis
Author & Adventurer

A Gathering
by
Marc Simmons

SUNSTONE PRESS
SANTA FE

All photographs and illustrations are from the author's collection unless otherwise indicated.

© 2008 by Marc Simmons. All Rights Reserved.

No part of this book may be reproduced in any form or by any electronic or mechanical means including information storage and retrieval systems without permission in writing from the publisher, except by a reviewer who may quote brief passages in a review.

Sunstone books may be purchased for educational, business, or sales promotional use. For information please write: Special Markets Department, Sunstone Press, P.O. Box 2321, Santa Fe, New Mexico 87504-2321.

Book design • Vicki Ahl
Body type • Bookman Old Style –•– Display type • Brush Script
Printed on acid free paper

Library of Congress Cataloging-in-Publication Data

Simmons, Marc.
  Charles F. Lummis : author and adventurer : a gathering / by Marc Simmons.
    p. cm.
  ISBN 978-0-86534-639-0 (hardcover : alk. paper) --
ISBN 978-0-86534-636-9 (softcover : alk. paper)
 1. Lummis, Charles Fletcher, 1859-1928. 2. Authors, American--19th century--Biography. 3. Authors, American--20th century--Biography. 4. Social reformers--United States--Biography. 5. Journalists--United States--Biography. 6. Southwestern States--Biography. I. Title.
  PS3523.U49Z79 2008
  818'.409--dc22
  [B]
                                                    2008034023

WWW.SUNSTONEPRESS.COM
SUNSTONE PRESS / POST OFFICE BOX 2321 / SANTA FE, NM 87504-2321 /USA
(505) 988-4418 / ORDERS ONLY (800) 243-5644 / FAX (505) 988-1025

*For
Amado and Ruth
and
To the Memory of
Consuelo Chaves Summers*

"Lummis, this tough little Yankee hero, is one against whom all subsequent Southwesterners must be measured. All hail Him!"

—Lawrence Clark Powell

Contents

Preface _____ 13

1 | Two Southwesterners:
    Charles F. Lummis and Amado Chaves _____ 23

2 | Cameras & Controversy _____ 71

3 | Lummis on Regional Books _____ 91

4 | Death of a Son: Amado Bandelier Lummis
       Tribute & Photo _____ 105

5 | The Death of Charles F. Lummis _____ 111

Preface

From the time I first read as a teenager *The Land of Poco Tiempo* by author Charles Fletcher Lummis (1859–1928), I became a fan of all his writings on the American Southwest, a collector of his books, and a student of his colorful life.

Knowing of my intense interest in Lummis, bookman Lawrence Clark Powell several times over the years urged me to undertake the writing of a comprehensive biography of the man. But other projects in the line of authorship always got in the way, and for the most part I left the writing up of Lummis' life to others. Notwithstanding, I have continued to acquire information, especially anecdotal material, about him.

In that endeavor, two people I came to know drew me closer to the real Charles F. Lummis. The first was Consuelo Chaves Summers, daughter of prominent political figure Amado Chaves, who became Lummis' best friend in New Mexico.

On his last two trips to the state, in 1926 and 1927 from his California home, Charles Lummis had spent some time at Amado's mountain ranch on the upper Pecos River. Mrs. Summers related to me from memory several humorous incidents she had witnessed during those visits.

Consuelo Chaves Summers, daughter of Amado Chaves at her Santa Fe, New Mexico home, 1968.

Subsequently, I had the opportunity to examine the surviving Amado Chaves papers, preserved in a large metal strongbox in his daughter Consuelo's basement. They contained previously unseen copies of correspondence between Lummis and Chaves, and those papers became the primary source I used in publishing the story of their friendship (1968). The little book, printed and released by E.W. Tedlock, Jr.'s San Marcos Press, bore the title *Two Southwesterners, Charles Lummis and Amado Chaves*. That now-rare material is included as Chapter 1 in this *Gathering*.

The second person who knew Charles F. Lummis intimately and who aided me in understanding his motivation and work was his youngest son Keith. Upon publication of *Two Southwesterners*, I sent a copy to Keith Lummis, whom I then did not know, and he responded from California with a warm letter of approval and thanks. That marked the beginning of our friendship.

Marc Simmons (right) with Keith Lummis at the Simmons ranch near Cerrillos, New Mexico, 1975.

Keith and his wife paid me several visits in New Mexico, where I showed him some historical sites closely identified with his father. When his sister Turbesé, who had long been working on a biography of Lummis, died in 1967 leaving the job incomplete, Keith took up the reins and finished the book himself. It was brought out by the University of Oklahoma Press in 1975, titled *Charles F. Lummis, The Man and His West*. My correspondence and occasional conversations with Keith Lummis continued up to the time of his death in 2001 at the age of 98.

The present book contains the text of *Two Southwesterners*, as well as an essay on Charles Lummis as a photographer, "Cameras & Controversy," which initially appeared in *New Mexico Magazine* (vol. 79, October 2001). To these have been added an original Lummis letter concerning books he considers basic for comprehending New Mexico's rich history and culture; a published tribute to his son who died at the age of six; and the first printed notice of Lummis' own death in 1928.

The author hopes that through this small volume the readers' curiosity will be aroused and might lead to exploring further the stimulating world of Charles F. Lummis.

1

Two Southwesterners

Two Southwesterners: Charles F. Lummis and Amado Chaves

On a blustery winter afternoon I knocked on the front door belonging to Mrs. Consuelo Chaves Summers, whose small house was only a few blocks from the main plaza in Santa Fe. At that moment my anticipation was about as keen as that of a detective on the point of uncovering an essential clue. For Mrs. Summers had invited me to join her in opening an ancient strongbox that contained the papers of her father Amado Chaves. As far as she was aware, the contents of the box had not been examined since her father's death some thirty-six years before.

For an historian, nothing offers more excitement than the chance to uncover and bring to light old documents. And the prospects seemed excellent that something of real value might emerge from the Chaves papers. One of the earliest members of the family to enter New Mexico had been Fernando Durán de Chaves, who served as an officer under the conquistador Don Diego de Vargas. His descendants distinguished themselves throughout the remainder of the colonial period, and one of them, Manuel Antonio Chaves, Mrs. Summers' grandfather, who was born just three years before Mexico achieved her independence from Spain, became a prominent statesman and noted Indian fighter. Whatever documents his eldest son Amado might have collected were sure to be of historical interest.

As Mrs. Summers answered my knock and led me through her parlor, she explained that the strongbox was kept in the basement so we would have to brave the dark and the cold. Before going down, however, she paused long enough to show me a curious relic that had belonged to her grandfather: a portion of a cane, the handle of which had been beautifully carved in dark wood and which merged into a pistol that slipped inside the staff. This ingenious weapon must have provided effective protection without being in the least conspicuous.

    In the basement Mrs. Summers produced an assortment of old keys and we began trying to match one of them with the padlock on the front of the chest. A half hour's work, however, proved that the task was hopeless. None would fit. Equally fruitless were our efforts to cut through the lock with file or hacksaw. The only solution seemed to be to lug the box to a locksmith and have an expert do the job. With considerable effort we maneuvered the chest step by step up into the daylight and onto the bed of my pickup truck. But our luck was still against us, for the locksmith was out for the rest of the day. His assistant, nevertheless, willingly gave us the use of a ring of 200 master keys, and Mrs. Summers and I stood in the street at the tail end of the truck and tried each and every one. When we failed again it began to appear as if the box was not meant to be opened that day. This was a case though where perseverance wins out, because at our next stop, a welding shop, we watched eagerly as a man with goggles and a torch sent the stubborn lock flying in a sputter of sparks.

We didn't touch the lid of the prized box until we had it home again and safely in Mrs. Summers' living room. Inside we found a great heap of papers and envelopes liberally garnished with cobwebs and salted with dust, testimony that the interior of the chest had not been disturbed in many years. As we waded through the treasure trove on that afternoon and the days which followed, it became clear that Amado Chaves had assembled a great many scraps of information concerning his family's history, no doubt with the intention of piecing it together some day into a coherent whole. Included in the collection were genealogical tables, personal notes and memorandums, clippings, and a large amount of correspondence including letters in Spanish from various members of the family containing their reminiscences. Here was much of the raw material of which history is made.

Amado Chaves

Of greatest interest to me was a bundle of letters to Amado Chaves from his good friend Charles Lummis, together with a fine collection of old photographic prints made by Lummis during a period extending over three decades. Of related interest were copies of several letters written by Chaves to various relatives and friends describing some of Lummis' strange quirks of behavior.

All of this material, amplified with supporting evidence from other pertinent sources, I have utilized in telling the story of the friendship of Charles Lummis and Amado Chaves. It is a tale that could not have been told until now. The importance of the narrative lies in the light it sheds on the career and character of one of the Southwest's most esteemed authors.

* * *

7

To all serious students of Southwestern history and culture, the name of Charles F. Lummis is familiar. An admirer once summed up Lummis' career by listing the occupations to which he had devoted himself: those of author, editor, explorer, barbarian, artist, archeologist and ethnologist, librarian, linguist, humanitarian, philanthropist, teacher, preacher, and entertainer.

With more than a dozen books to his credit, Lummis during his lifetime won a national following, attracting readers who delighted in his exotic tales of the American Southwest. His style mirrored his personality—flinty, virile, earnest. In swift flashing strokes he could bring to the printed page as lucidly as anyone has yet done, the full flavor and feeling of that vast country stretching from New Mexico to the California coast.

Portrait of Charles F. Lummis in his middle years.

Apart from his writings, Lummis is best remembered for his role in the founding of the Southwest Museum in Los Angeles and the School of American Research in Santa Fe, his spirited defense of the American Indian, and his successful campaign for the preservation of California's Spanish missions.

A man of Lummis' energy and talent had the opportunity to meet and associate with many prominent personalities and, in fact, he took pride in numbering among his close friends such luminaries as Theodore Roosevelt, Will Rogers, novelist Jack London, and Mrs. John C. Fremont, wife of the Pathfinder. But of all his friends and acquaintances, none occupied in his life and thoughts a place comparable to that of Amado Chaves.

It is difficult to imagine any two men more unalike in background and temperament—Lummis, the pugnacious New Englander; Chaves, the soft-spoken descendant of Spanish aristocracy—and yet they formed a warm friendship that endured for almost forty years.

In 1884, Lummis, an aspiring and

bumptious young newspaper man, accepted an assignment as editor of the *Los Angeles Times*. To reach his new employment he walked the entire distance from Chillicothe, Ohio, to Los Angeles, a distance of 3,507 miles. The story of this extraordinary hike with its attendant adventures he related in the book *A Tramp Across the Continent.*

It was on this trip that Charles Lummis entered the Territory of New Mexico for the first time and, like artists, writers, and other sensitive persons to this day, was captivated by the stark and awesome landscape and by the color and charm of the native inhabitants, both Spanish and Indian. He discovered a fascinating and totally new world—a world that would soon provide him with an abundance of material for his books. In later years Lummis, when he had become a resident of California, still referred to New Mexico affectionately as "my own country."

Part of the attraction which he felt toward the Territory in that year of 1884 must have stemmed from a five day rest he enjoyed at the hacienda of the Chaves family located near the small village of San Mateo north of Grants. Leaving the main California route, Lummis hitched a ride on a wagon, and late on a cold winter's evening reached the Chaves ranch.

The purpose of this side trip was to make the acquaintance of a man about whom Lummis had heard much during the previous few weeks—Don Manuel Antonio Chaves, the aged patriarch of the family and the man whom the *peones* of New Mexico had nicknamed *Leoncito*, the Little Lion, because of his prowess in wars against hostile Navajos. It was the fame of this frontier fighter that had lured Lummis to San Mateo. Nor was he to be disappointed. For Don Manuel proved to be one of those few men who were equal to the reputation ascribed to them by their contemporaries, and he was just the sort who appealed to the romantic mind of the young Lummis.

With a hospitality that was traditional in nineteenth century New Mexico, the house of Chaves opened its doors to the strange wayfarer from the East. Lummis, always responsive to the unusual, explored the canyons and mesas on the ranch by day and by night joined in the family circle with its legends, songs, and games of old Spain.

During his idyllic but brief stay at San Mateo, Lummis came to revere old Manuel Chaves as a father whom he described as "a courtly Spanish gentleman, brave as a lion, tender as a woman, spotless of honor, modest as heroic ... who seldom spoke of his own achievements." The elder Chaves at this time, however, was approaching the end of his life, suffering from wounds sustained in over a half century of bitter warfare with nomadic Indians. If the youthful Lummis held Don Manuel as a father, it was the eldest son, Amado, who became a brother and remained a steadying influence throughout the rest of his life.

The aged Indian fighter Manuel A. Chaves, as Lummis knew him in his last years before his death, 1889.

When they first met, Amado Chaves was eight years the senior. In character he was the image of his father, though perhaps somewhat more given to intellectual pursuits. As a youth, he had been sent east for an education—Don Manuel had dispatched an armed guard to accompany him as far as St. Louis as protection against family enemies—and in 1876, Amado had received a law degree from the National University Law School in Washington. His diploma had been personally presented by Ulysses S. Grant. The law career had to be postponed, however, since the burden of managing the family hacienda devolved upon his shoulders as his father's health declined. In Charles Lummis, Amado found a man of considerable learning and nimble wit whose lively interest in all things Spanish helped cement a strong bond of friendship.

Lummis resumed his journey and eventually reached California and his job as editor of the *Los Angeles Times*. Fate, nevertheless, decided that his immediate destiny belonged to New Mexico. Within three years he was struck down by a paralytic stroke brought on by overwork. In the account of his illness, Lummis declares he resolved at this point to "go to the wilderness and live outdoors till I'm well; and off I packed to New Mexico, though barely able to waddle. Me to the old Santa Fe Trail."

And it was straight to the Chaves hacienda that he headed, to be welcomed by his "princely friend Don Amado." Since he could scarcely walk and his speech was affected, his host decided the logical place for him was bed, but plucky Lummis would have none of that. With his one good arm, he shouldered a shotgun and spent his days hunting cottontails.

By spring he was well enough to help in the sheep camps and join the cowhands on the round-up. And within time he began making extended jaunts into the mesa wilderness with a ponderous camera on his shoulder. It is from this period that many of Lummis' incomparable photographs of New Mexico have come down to us.

Scene in Puerto del Aire Canyon of central New Mexico.

Lummis' recovery received a major setback when he suffered a second stroke after a year on the Chaves estate. It was his determination to "prove that he was greater than anything that could happen to him," which won the profound admiration of Amado Chaves, as well as all others who knew him at this difficult time. When Lummis could muster the strength, he was back to his old routine of photographing or excavating and plotting Indian ruins, often with friend Amado or a younger brother, Ireneo, at his side. Once to prove his mettle, he crawled a hundred feet into the cave of a mountain lion with a single-barreled shotgun and a torch in his teeth. Fortunately for his future career the lion was not at home and he emerged to confront a white-faced and badly shaken Don Amado.

When his health permitted, Lummis moved to Isleta Pueblo in the Rio Grande Valley and began collecting Tiwa Indian folk tales. On a visit to his old haunts around San Mateo one Holy Week, he was able to secure twenty-five photographs of the strange activities of the Penitente sect, including several views of a mock crucifixion. This extraordinary feat was accomplished not without considerable risk. The details of his friend's adventure were outlined long afterward by Amado Chaves, who wrote:

"Lummis was determined to photograph the Penitentes. The morada is in a little side canyon off the San Mateo Canyon about one half mile from the village. A short distance from the morada is a hill on top of which the Penitentes had put a large cross. During Holy Week they had two men on that hill to prevent any stranger from going near the morada to see the Penitentes when they were in their exercises. My brother, Ireneo, knowing that it was dangerous for Lummis to go alone, went with him. He put on his belt with his pistol and Lummis put his instruments on his shoulder. When they arrived at the hill, the guards stopped them. They told Lummis that if he attempted to go to the morada they would break his photographic instruments and if necessary they would break his head.

"Ireneo told them that he was going and that if anyone attempted to hurt him or the instruments, he would blow his head off. They saw his pistol and then he made them march ahead to the morada. When they arrived, there was a man tied on the cross. A group were marching and whipping themselves. Some of this group were carrying heavy crosses. The man on the cross was fainting, so they brought him down and soon revived him. Lummis noted the number of minutes that he was on the cross. He made a complete set of photographs and sent them to *Scribner's Magazine*. They were published and somebody sent a copy of the magazine to the Penitentes. They were furious and determined to finish him off in some way."

The Penitente pictures, which were later included in his book *The Land of Poco Tiempo*, were among the most unusual ever made by Lummis and they did almost cost him his life. In a vengeful mood, the members of the San Mateo sect purportedly ambushed him on several occasions, but each time scored a near miss. Then on Valentine's Day of the following year as Lummis emerged from his house at Isleta Pueblo, a hidden assailant gravely wounded him with a load of buckshot fired at close range.

The Penitente village of San Mateo, New Mexico.

For a description of the events leading up to the shooting and of what followed, we again rely on Amado Chaves:

"Lummis had located at the Pueblo of Isleta where he had a nice clean room. All the Indians liked him very much and he was very good to the children. Every time he went to Albuquerque he would take them a bag of candy.

"He always worked until after two o'clock in the morning writing. For this he paid bitterly. One night when the moon was full at one o'clock he opened the door of his room to go out for a stretch when some man from behind the small adobe wall in front of the house fired at him with a shotgun. He fell down but got quickly up and started with his rifle after the fellow. He saw him running but his eyes got full of blood and he fell down. His neighbors who heard the shot followed him, picked him up and put him in bed.

"Early in the morning, a telegram was sent to me at Grants in care of our old friend, a merchant there, Sol Bibo. He at once started a man on a fast horse to San Mateo to bring me the telegram. As soon as I received it I jumped on my horse and started for Grants. When I arrived there Sol Bibo and I took the first train for Isleta.

A Penitente procession near San Mateo, New Mexico.

"We found Lummis in bed. The Indians had extracted fourteen buckshot and covered his wounds with clean white rags. We tried our best to take him to the hospital in Albuquerque where a doctor would do something for him. But he would not go as he detested doctors. He said the Indians would cure him."

With careful nursing Lummis recovered from his wounds, but he carried some of the buckshot under his hide to the end of his days. The superstitious Penitentes apparently decided that their intended victim, having escaped several assassination attempts, must be something of a wizard, and that it would be best to abandon their quest for revenge.

Later Lummis boasted that on a return visit to San Mateo he was able to break down the hostility of the Penitentes and win their guarded friendship. This accomplishment seems less remarkable than the fact that he himself held no grudge and that he seemed to treat the attempts against his life as a matter of small consequence.

In 1892 Lummis accompanied his friend and colleague, the Swiss archeologist Adolph Bandelier on a scientific expedition to South America. By 1894 he was back in Los Angeles where he launched into a new set of projects including the construction of his famous home, El Alisal. With a wife and family—he had earlier married the school marm at Isleta Pueblo—and with several books still to compose, Lummis sunk his roots and for the most part spent his remaining years at tasks in California. Writing to Amado in New Mexico, he confessed, "If I were a *soltero* (bachelor) it is probable I should never settle down in civilization till too old to be *vagamundearado*; but the family and home are better than roving."

Lummis' wife and home at Isleta Pueblo.

On November 15 of 1894, a first son was born and was christened Amado Bandelier Lummis. Three years later the proud father dedicated a new book of collected stories entitled *The Enchanted Burro* to: "Amado and Amado, The Name That Stood for Such a Friend is Tall Enough for Two—." Tragically, the younger Amado died of pneumonia on Christmas day, 1900, at the age of six.

Over the years Lummis and Chaves kept up a correspondence. Often in the preparation of a new book or article, Lummis would consult his friend regarding an obscure point of history or the regional meaning of some Spanish word. For example, he once wrote to Amado:

> "... Here is something that I really need to know. The word 'chaparro' is very loosely used—and you know my mania for having things Exact.
>
> "It is generally used in the Southwest for any big bush, and a 'chaparral' for a region or area covered with any big shrubs. But I have a vague

idea that its proper use in New Mexico at least, is for a specific kind of shrub. Is it scrub-oak or what?"

Upon this and similar requests the affable and always courteous Don Amado made available to Lummis his own first hand knowledge of the Hispanic Southwest.

In precisely what manner Amado Chaves viewed his strange friend is difficult to judge at this date. He once remarked, however, "that Lummis was very eccentric," but then he charitably added, "like so many geniuses are!" Chaves possessed a rich store of anecdotes concerning Lummis' unusual behavior and with the slightest prodding he could be moved to relate some amusing story. Perhaps his favorite concerned a visit to the White House, the details of which Chaves summarized in a letter to an acquaintance:

"I am now going to give you an incident in Lummis' life that I doubt whether there is anyone but myself who can. On his way back from Washington from his visit to Colonel

Roosevelt, he stopped to see me and gave me a fresh account of all that happened.

"He was always a good friend of the Indians. An American doctor in California bought an old Spanish land grant and it was approved by the government's Land Court as complete and perfect. It was ordered surveyed and when that was done it was found that a tribe of Indians was living inside the boundaries of the grant.

"Many agents who had been sent to investigate matters had evidently been bought by somebody, and their reports did not favor the Indians. The doctor started litigation to force them off his land. The Court sustained his claim and issued an order to evict the Indians from their homes. It was then that Lummis wrote a very violent article against any government that would permit such an injustice. The article was published in the *Los Angeles Times* and it was brought to the attention of Colonel Roosevelt who was President at that time. He knew he could not rely on the reports on file in the Department so he sent a telegram to his old friend Lummis to come to Washington at once to have a talk with him to see what could be done for these Indians.

"Lummis at once packed his baggage. It was a buckskin saddle bag that opened in the center and on the ends it had fringes. In it he put his few articles of clothing, a shirt, pijamas, and a pair of socks and a couple of handkerchiefs. He took the first train for Washington. On his arrival there at the R.R. station he went to the lunch counter where he ordered ham and eggs and TWO cups of coffee. He was a great coffee drinker. He never drank less than nine cups a day and sometimes more.

"After eating breakfast he rolled a cigarette and started on foot for the White House. When he arrived there he was met by the door keeper who conducted him to the ante room where there was a crowd waiting their turn to see the President. The women were beautifully dressed and some of the men had silk hats. Lummis was dressed as usual: Indian moccasins, green corduroy suit, flannel shirt, Indian belt, red handkerchief around his neck and a big sombrero."

(Shortly after the events described here, Lummis accompanied Roosevelt to dinner attired in this same colorful raiment. A newspaper reporter was heard to inquire, "Mr. Lummis, I should think you'd change your dress when dining with the President of the United States," whereupon he was hit with this stinging rejoinder: "Don't change my face when I dine with the President. Why should I change my clothes?")

"He handed his card to the door keeper telling him he wanted to see Colonel Roosevelt. He took a chair and while waiting he proceeded to roll a cigarette. He never used store cigarettes. He used brown paper and carried a small bag with tobacco. To light his cigarette he carried a piece of steel or flint and a rag that had been treated with gunpowder. While he was doing that a tall, handsome young man, blond, elegantly dressed came towards him. He had in his hand Lummis' card. He stopped with it in front of Lummis and said, 'I believe you are Mr. Lummis.'

"Then Lummis said in a voice of thunder,

'Yes, I am Mr. Lummis and you must be Colonel Roosevelt, President of the United States.'

"All the people who were waiting there looked at him with wide eyes. The young man said, 'I am not Colonel Roosevelt.' But before he could utter anything else, Lummis said, 'If you are not Colonel Roosevelt, I would like to know what in the hell you are doing with my card. I sent it to him and not to you.'

"The young man then replied, 'It is this way, Mr. Lummis. Many good people come here thinking that they have business with the President, but really their business is with some other department. If they tell me their business, I can direct them to the right place and save them and the President valuable time.'

"Lummis then said in a very loud voice so that all could hear him, 'Young man, please give that card to Colonel Roosevelt and tell him that Mr. Lummis from California is here and wishes to see him. That he has no business with the President or anybody else in Washington and that if the President has no business with him, he would like to know it so he can go right back from here to the railroad station where he came from and take the first train for California.'

"In the meantime, his cigarette had gone out and he took out his fire making outfit to light it again. The people all over the ante room were looking at him in great astonishment. They likely thought he was a wild man from the plains. The young man then left and told the President what Lummis had said. In a minute or two you could hear loud cheerful laughter in the President's private office.

"Colonel Roosevelt himself came to the door and when he saw Lummis, he called out, 'Come here old fellow, and quick.' Lummis jumped up and putting his baggage on his shoulder ran toward the President. Colonel Roosevelt grabbed his hand and gave him a hearty shake and embraced him and took him to his office. He kept him an hour talking over the Indian situation. The result was that a commission of three men was appointed to find a suitable tract of government land with water to give the Indians. The Commission, of which Lummis was chairman, went to work and found a splendid tract of unoccupied land, had it surveyed, and sent in their report to the President who got busy and had an act passed by Congress donating the land to the Indians. It contains eight times more land than they ever had before and ten times more water. The Indians were moved and were helped to build new houses, and now they have perfect title, all due to Lummis and the great Colonel Roosevelt."

While Lummis was building his career in California after 1900, Amado Chaves was advancing his own in New Mexico. In the years following the death of his father Colonel Manuel Chaves in 1889, Amado resided in Albuquerque and Santa Fe or on property which was acquired along the Upper Pecos River in the Sangre de Cristo Mountains.

Facing page: Charles Lummis' *mecha,* **Spanish fire-making wick, used with flint-and-steel. Fancy silver stopper on chain at top was used to plug the tube and put out the burning wick. Leather carrying thong is at right. Lummis acquired the artifact in Peru while there with Bandelier, 1892–1893.**

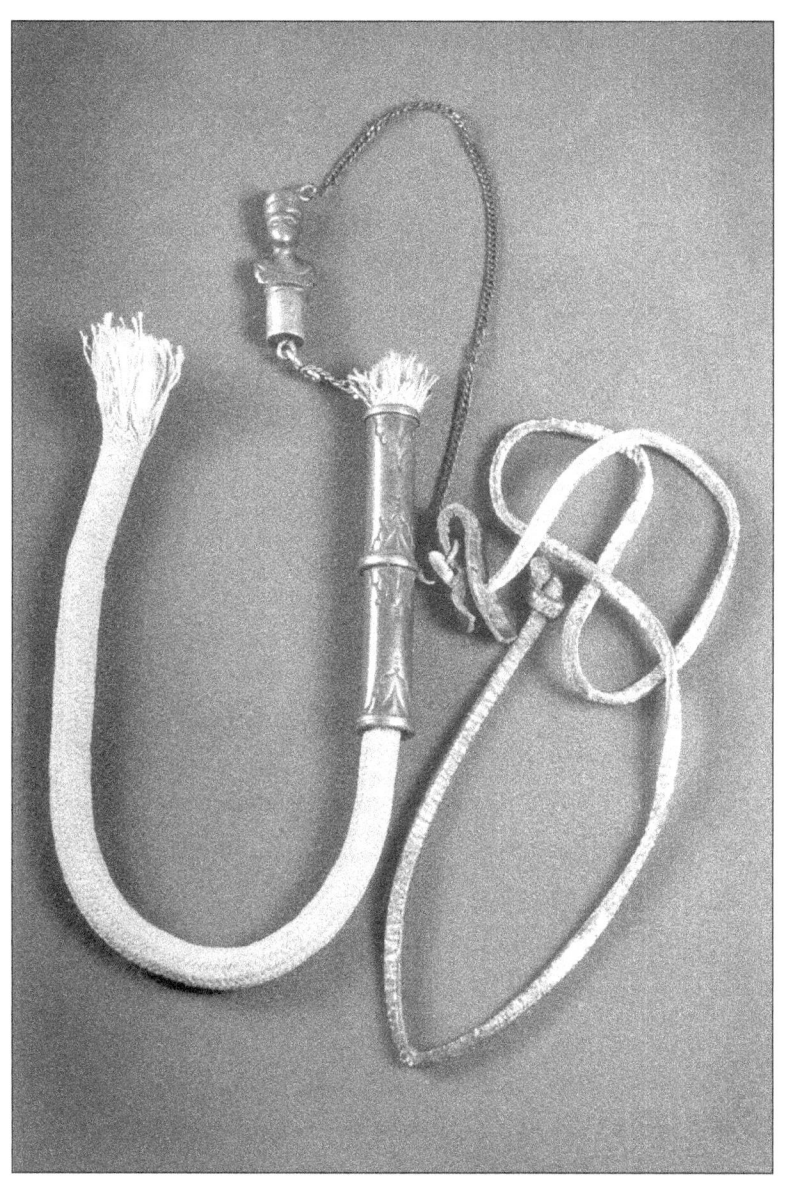

In 1891 he became the first Superintendent of Public Instruction for the Territory of New Mexico and was the moving figure in a program to bring educational benefits to isolated Spanish-speaking communities. In the same year, he was elected mayor of the city of Santa Fe and in 1903 he became a senator in the territorial council. During this period of political activity, he had married and undertaken the responsibility of raising a family.

From time to time, Don Amado had word from his old companion of former days. In 1917 Lummis wrote caustically of his recent role as adviser to dramatic productions:

"The play of *Ramona* was miserably done, against my advice. They consulted me, and then did everything exactly as I told them not to. ... The Movie People are on the average the most conscienceless pirates I have ever met—and as you know I know the frontier, you can understand that I am saying something pretty strong. I have had experience with them in quite a number of cases—including *Ramona* and the *Penitentes* and various other things—some of which they summoned me to advise them about at their studios, and some of which they staged here at my home. And of all the pirates I ever encountered, they take the loot."

In the early 1920s Amado Chaves, now over seventy, spent several winters at La Jolla, California to escape the cold thin air of New Mexico. He was able to visit Lummis frequently, and the writer, himself now a graybeard, often spoke of returning to New Mexico for a final round of visits to people and places he had known in his youth.

Lummis' poor health, however, seemed to preclude the realization of any such hope. He had undergone a cataract operation in 1923, but it had provided only temporary relief for his failing eyesight. In spite of this, and other equally serious ailments, he continued to write and in the midst of his afflictions was able to revise and expand for publication an older work which was reissued under the title of *Mesa, Cañon and Pueblo*.

On a visit to Camulos Rancho, California.
Left to right: Jordan Lummis (called Quimu,
his Isleta Indian name, by his family); Bertha,
Charles F. Lummis' eldest daughter; Amado Chaves,
who often visited Charles F. Lummis in California;
Turbesé, Charles F. Lummis' youngest daughter;
and Charles F. Lummis.

Finally in 1926 Lummis felt strong enough to undertake the long-planned trip to New Mexico. In all he spent some five weeks touring his old haunts, viewing the Indian ceremonial at Gallup, and renewing acquaintances at Acoma, Santa Clara, and Isleta Pueblos where he had photographed and collected folktales thirty-five years before. Time was even mustered for a lecture to the impressionable Harvey Girls at the La Fonda Hotel in Santa Fe.

With all the round of activities, Lummis still found time for two weeks with Amado Chaves and his children on the Upper Pecos River. At a later time Don Amado told with amusement of journeying to Santa Fe to pick up his guest.

"I told Katherine (his eldest daughter) ... not to load the car because when Lummis travels he carries a lot of baggage. She thought that I was joking. He was stopping in a little hotel by the name of Savoy on Galisteo Street. When we called for him there was a large pile of baggage in front of the hotel. When the manager of the hotel saw us, I noticed that he commenced to smile. Katherine asked Lummis to point out which were his things and we would put them in the car. He said that all that pile belonged to him, and we piled it in and on the outside of the car as best we could."

Apparently the salubrious air of the New Mexico high country was of great benefit to Lummis' spirits. Almost blind now, he could, nevertheless, go trout fishing in the rushing mountain streams and putter with mortar and stone in the building of a fireplace in Chaves' log cabin.

The adventure so agreed with him that he was able to carry out a similar but shorter trip the following year. And he apparently planned to return each summer thereafter. "Please God we may meet another year," he wrote to Amado, "for I fully intend to make annual pilgrimages to my New Mexico. Every year makes Los Angeles crazier and more crowded, but New Mexico is a bit of God's Grace in making a land so spacious (and so dry) that the hand of man shall never destroy it, nor much disfigure."

In Lummis' last letter to his old companion written just a short time before his death in 1928, he showed himself to be the same man of courage and determination who had hiked across the Southwest almost five decades before. "There is no human probability that I shall ever be able to visit my New Mexico any more, but I am getting along very nicely and am entirely happy and trying to get a whole lot done."

Charles Lummis is best remembered in New Mexico today for his books on the region's history and folklore. In their own way these works still are regarded as minor classics. He was the first to bring the Southwestern United States to the attention of provincial-minded Easterners, and when he instructed them in his writings to "See America First" he was thinking specifically in terms of the scenic wonders and delightful customs offered by New Mexico.

For Lummis, Amado Chaves represented all that was fine and noble in the Spanish tradition. Proud, diligent, loyal, and generous to a fault, Chaves stood by the aggressive and flamboyant Lummis through fair weather and foul. Both men had the good fortune to experience these exciting and lusty years during which the American Southwest was coming of age, and each in his own way contributed in no small measure to the area's progress. Destiny perhaps first brought them together in 1884, but it was strength of character on both sides which welded their friendship for forty years.

Facing page: Lummis on one of his last visits to New Mexico, 1926, posing with Cherokee singer Tsianina Blackstone and Santiago Naranjo, Indian governor of Santa Clara pueblo.

Here is a list of books by Charles Lummis, including books written about him and an article by Amado Chaves.

Books by Charles Lummis:

A New Mexico David and other Stories and Sketches of the Southwest. New York: Scribner's, 1891.

A Tramp Across the Continent. New York: Scribner's, 1892.

Some Strange Corners of Our Country. New York: Century: 1892.

The Land of Poco Tiempo. New York: Scribner's, 1893. New edition by the University of New Mexico Press, 1966.

The Spanish Pioneers. Chicago: A.C. McClurg, 1893. Reprinted by the Rio Grande Press.

Los Exploradores Españoles del Siglo XVI. A translation of *The Spanish Pioneers* published first in Barcelona in 1916, then in Madrid in 1960.

The King of the Broncos and Other Stories of New Mexico. New York: Scribner's, 1897.

The Enchanted Burro and Other Stories. Chicago: A.C. McClurg, 1897.

Pueblo Indian Folk Stories. New York: Century, 1910.

My Friend Will. Chicago: A.C. McClurg, 1911. A new edition by the Cultural Assets Press, Los Angeles, 1961.

Mesa, Cañon and Pueblo. New York: Century, 1925. An expanded version of *Some Strange Corners of Our Country.*

A Bronco Pegasus. Boston: Houghton Mifflin, 1928. Collected verses.

Flowers of Our Lost Romance. Boston: Houghton Mifflin, 1929.

General Crook and the Apache Wars. Flagstaff: Northland Press, 1966.

Bullying the Moqui, Charles F. Lummis' Defense of the Hopi Indians. Edited by Robert Easton and Mackenzie Brown. Prescott, Arizona: Prescott College Press, 1968.

The Southwestern Wonderland. Albuquerque: Vinegar Tom Press, n.d.

Dateline Fort Bowie: Charles Fletcher Lummis Reports on an Apache War. Edited by Dan L. Thrapp. Norman: University of Oklahoma Press, 1979.

Letters from the Southwest, 1884-1885. Edited by James W. Byrkit. Tucson: University of Arizona Press, 1989.

Books about Charles Lummis

Jane Apostol, *El Alisal, Where History Lingers*. Los Angeles: Historical Society of Southern California. History of the residence, El Alisal, that Lummis himself built in Los Angeles.

Edwin R. Bingham, *Charles F. Lummis, Editor of the Southwest*. San Marino, California, 1955.

J. Manuel Espinosa (ed.), "Some Charles F. Lummis Letters, 1897-1903," *New Mexico Quarterly Review*, XI (1941), 147-66.

Turbesé Lummis Fiske and Keith Lummis, *Charles F. Lummis, The Man and His West*. Norman: University of Oklahoma Press: 1975.

Dudley Gordon, *Charles F. Lummis, Crusader in Corduroy*. Los Angeles: Cultural Assets Press, 1972.

Edgar L. Hewett, "Lummis the Inimitable," Papers of the School of American Research, Santa Fe, 1944.

Patrick T. Houlihan and Betsy E. Houlihan, *Lummis in the Pueblos*. Flagstaff, Arizona: Northland Press, 1986. Photographs by Lummis.

Mark Thompson, *American Character: The Curious Life of Charles Fletcher Lummis and the Rediscovery of the Southwest*. New York: Arcade Publishing, 2001.

Article by Amado Chaves

The Defeat of the Comanches in 1716. Historical Society of New Mexico, Publications in History, Vol. 8, 1906.

2

Cameras & Controversy

Cameras & Controversy

Of all the early photographers who aimed their large box cameras at enchanting New Mexican scenes, Charles Fletcher Lummis was without a doubt the most eccentric and versatile. Actually, he remains better known today as an author, historian, journalist, preservationist and Indian-rights advocate than he does as an accomplished picture maker.

For more than 40 years, I have followed and studied the career of the mercurial Lummis (pronounced *Lum*, not *Loom*) and interviewed old-timers who remembered his last visits to New Mexico prior to his death in 1928. A New Englander by birth and educated at Harvard, the young Charles first saw the Southwest in 1884–1885 when he hiked across the country on his way to a new job at the *Los Angeles Times*.

His initial encounter with New Mexico's Indian and Hispanic cultures would prove to be, for him, a defining experience. As he fell under their spell, he resolved to write about the exotic people who dwelled in "the land of *poco tiempo*," which became the title of one of his books on New Mexican folk and folkways.

After three years on the Los Angeles paper as city editor, keeping a brutal schedule of 20-hour workdays, Lummis suffered a stroke resulting in paralysis of his left side and arm.

To recuperate, he headed back to New Mexico, the one place that appealed to him most on his original tramp to California. There he had made friends who were now willing to take in the convalescent. It was the forepart of 1888 when he reached the ranch of aging Colonel Manuel Chaves and his sons, located near the village of San Mateo in the shadow of Mount Taylor.

During his several-month stay and as part of his rehabilitation program, Lummis turned to photography. By necessity, he used what was available in that day: a cumbersome 40-pound view camera supported on a tripod that took 5-inch by 8-inch glass negatives. The weight and bulk of such equipment might have daunted an ordinary man, but Lummis accepted it as just one more challenge that might contribute to his recovery.

His earliest-known pictures are ones he made that summer: ranch scenes, views of San Mateo and nearby San Rafael, and portraits of some of the villagers.

Among the latter was a photograph of a 17-year-old girl, her mother and aunt, all reputed by local gossips to be confirmed witches. Ignoring warnings about his own safety, Lummis persuaded the three women, through flattery and good humor, to pose for his camera in front of their door.

Facing page: In 1888 Lummis persuaded three professed witches at the village of San Rafael to pose for his camera.

His hunger for the sensational and flair for the dramatic drew Lummis into a confrontation with the Hermanos de Luz, a lay religious brotherhood popularly known as the Penitentes. Their customs, indeed their very existence, were virtually unknown in 1888 outside the boundaries of New Mexico.

Once Lummis learned that during Holy Week the Penitentes lashed themselves with whips, tied cactus pads to their bare backs and staged a mock crucifixion in which one of the brothers was tied to a cross, he was determined to capture it all on film.

The Chaves family attempted to dissuade him from carrying out his foolish plans, but Lummis would not be deterred. So in the end, one of Chaves' sons and a ranch hand, both armed with pistols, accompanied him as bodyguards.

On Holy Thursday, Lummis set up his tripod and camera on a hill overlooking the Penitentes' procession route. While taking pictures with his one good arm, his own Colt rested on top of the box camera, where it would be handy in case of need. Afterward he admitted that his brazen intrusion had caused "a great deal of bad feeling" and produced "many threats" against him.

The following day, Good Friday, Lummis and his guards showed up at the *morada*, or Penitente chapter house, as preparations were under way for the "crucifixion." As he later wrote, "We had to wedge through a scowling and threatening mob."

Before a disturbance could start, the head Penitente (called *hermano mayor*) emerged from the *morada* and calmed matters by drawing an 8-foot square on the ground. He told Lummis to stay inside the lines, and if he photographed from there, he would not be bothered.

**Facing page:
Hermano Mayor of the Penitente sect at San Mateo.**

Hermano Mayor of the Penitente sect at San Mateo.

A remarkable series of images was caught by Lummis' camera that day. Included was a startling picture of a figure suspended on the cross, his head hidden by a black hangman's cap. Son Keith Lummis once told me that of the thousands of photographs his father took, that was probably the one of which he was most proud.

Lummis sent them, with an accompanying article to 17 Eastern magazines and all mailed back rejection slips. Having never heard of the New Mexican Penitentes, the editors assumed that the article was a fabrication and the illustrations were fakes. Finally, *Cosmopolitan* magazine bought and printed the submission.

Lummis published a revised text and two of the photographs in several of his subsequent books. He always claimed that he was the first to bring the Penitentes to the notice of the world—and the only one who ever photographed their "supreme rites." He almost paid for that privilege with his life, as it turned out.

Late in 1888, Lummis bid the Chaveses

goodbye and moved eastward to Isleta Pueblo, renting a room in the village for $2.50 a month. He intended to learn the ways of the Indians and photograph them to boot. His uneasy residency there would stretch into three years.

The same pushy attitude that the Yankee interloper had displayed toward the Penitentes now became the problem of the Isletans. While he established close friendships with a number of individual Indians, the village elders dropped hints that he should go. Lummis ignored the signals and stayed.

But the pueblo had a larger problem than Lummis, who was no more than a minor irritant. Government agents had forcibly removed a number of children from their parents and placed them in the U.S. Indian School in Albuquerque. Outraged, Lummis denounced it as kidnapping.

He engaged a lawyer, composed blistering columns for the newspapers and drummed up public support. The government had no better luck than the Penitentes at reining in the stubborn Lummis. It capitulated.

In triumph, Lummis led an Isleta delegation to the Indian School, where the "captive" youngsters were released and brought home to the waiting arms of their families. Thereafter, he and his camera enjoyed unhindered access to the pueblo.

In his quarters, he rigged up a darkroom to do his own one-handed developing. While at Isleta, he was using the relatively simple and inexpensive cyanotype process that produced deep-blue photographic prints. Distilled water was required in mixing the chemicals, but lacking that, he resorted to Río Grande water, brought by Isleta women on their heads in *tinajas*. It contaminated his chemicals and resulted in the fading and spotting of many of his photos.

Late one night, Lummis emerged from his room into the moonlight and was felled by a shotgun blast from an unknown assassin. Eve Douglas, sister-in-law of the Anglo operator of the local trading post, was summoned to bind up his wounds. She nursed him back to health, and soon afterward they were married.

Lummis at Isleta Pueblo, May 1894, with wife Eve, daughter Turbesé, and Indian boy Luís Abeita.

The identity of the shooter was never established, but Lummis had his own theory. He contended that the Penitentes, upon being shown a copy of the *Cosmopolitan* article, vowed vengeance and hired someone to gun him down. Actually, he had made a number of enemies, so his accusation against the Penitentes seems less plausible today.

Upon recovering, Lummis made several photographic visits to Acoma, a place that fascinated him. Once while camped near there, a heavy-set man in a black suit walked up to his fire. He introduced himself as Adolph F. Bandelier, archaeologist and historian. The chance meeting launched a lifelong friendship.

Lummis became Bandelier's assistant and student. Together, they pursued research opportunities across New Mexico. "We always went by foot," Lummis recalled later, "my big camera and glass plates in my knapsack, the heavy tripod under my arm."

A dance at Acoma Indian pueblo.

Charles F. Lummis never pretended to be an art photographer. Critics often dismissed his images for their poor composition and lack of taste in subject matter. But Lummis himself acknowledged those deficiencies. His primary aim was to capture moments in time for the historical record.

An elder of Acoma pueblo.

The Lummis home, El Alisal, under construction on the edge of Los Angeles. Isleta Indians came by train from New Mexico to help with the work. Lummis died here in 1928.

In his last years, he expressed pleasure that so many of his early pictures were unique, preserving faces of colorful types that had disappeared, or buildings that had been destroyed, or ceremonies that were no more. In that, as he well knew, lay his legacy as a Southwestern photographer.

3

Lummis on Regional Books

Lummis on Regional Books

T he original copy of the interesting letter that follows came into my possession a number of years ago. In it Charles F. Lummis answers an inquiry made in 1908 by Professor D.M. Richards of the University of New Mexico, Albuquerque. The professor was seeking to assemble a small collection of basic books on New Mexico for the school, which had allotted him only fifty dollars for the task. At that time the institution had no formal library, and indeed would not obtain its first library building until 1926.

For advice in accomplishing his mission, Professor Richards had approached the right person. Then, Lummis was the chief librarian for the City of Los Angeles, he had published seven books on the Southwest and was a recognized expert on the archeology and history of the region.

Guardedly in this letter he recommends certain books, while others he condemns in rather acerbic terms. Throughout, he provides Richards only with the last name of authors, and usually no more than a shortened title, or sometimes no title at all for the book.

Here is the original letter. I have searched out the full titles and the authors' complete names, listing them as "The Charles F. Lummis Book List" in the order that they appear in the Lummis letter following the reproduction of the letter.

The Southwest Society,
Archæological Institute of America

PRESIDENT, J. O. KOEPFLI
VICE-PRESIDENTS
GEN. H. G. OTIS   H. W. O'MELVENY   DR. NORMAN BRIDGE
TREASURER, W. C. PATTERSON   CURATOR, DR. F. M. PALMER   SECRETARY, CHAS. F. LUMMIS
EXECUTIVE COMMITTEE
CHARLES CASSATT DAVIS   JOSEPH SCOTT   MARY E. FOY
WM. H. BURNHAM   JOHN D. BICKNELL   J. A. FOSHAY
BURT ESTES HOWARD   J. A. MUNK   J. H. MARTINDALE
F. M. PALMER   CHAS. F. LUMMIS
JAMES SLAUSON

Los Angeles, Cal. Mar. 4th, 1908.

Prof. D. M. Richards,
    University of New Mexico,
        Albuquerque, N.M.

My dear Prof. Richards:

    I have a list made out for you, with the approximate prices of each work--- though $50 would not go far in making a reference department of the history of your own territory.

    Bancroft's New Mexico is probably the best of all his dreary series; and is indispensable. Prince's is worse than worthless. Miss Haines's and Prof. Ladd's are poor truck. You will have to beg, borrow, buy or steal all of Bandelier's works. This will be difficult, for all of them are out of print. No serious New Mexican Institution can get along without the works of the foremost authority on New Mexico and the greatest scholar that ever lived in the territory. I would suggest that you write to W. H. Lowdermilk, F. St., Washington, D.C.; Burrows Bros., Cleveland, O., and other dealers in America asking them to secure for you the Historical Introduction, "The Contributions" and the two volumes of the "Final Report", and "Mexico".

    I think you will also need to have two of my own books--- "The Land of Poco Tiempo" and "The Spanish Pioneers". I am sorry to have to recommend them; but there is distressingly little

The Southwest Society,
Archæological Institute of America

PRESIDENT, J. O. KOEPFLI
VICE-PRESIDENTS
GEN. H. G. OTIS   H. W. O'MELVENY   DR. NORMAN BRIDGE
TREASURER, W. C. PATTERSON   CURATOR, DR. F. M. PALMER   SECRETARY, CHAS. F. LUMMIS
EXECUTIVE COMMITTEE
CHARLES CASSATT DAVIS   JOSEPH SCOTT   MARY E. FOY
WM. H. BURNHAM   JOHN D. BICKNELL   J. A. FOSHAY
BURT ESTES HOWARD   J. A. MUNK   J. H. MARTINDALE
F. M. PALMER   CHAS. F. LUMMIS
JAMES SLAUSON

Prof. R.-2.   Los Angeles, Cal.

historical work on New Mexico that is not worse than worthless. Of course, you will have to have Kendall, Gregg, W.W.H.Davis, Bartlett, (personal narrative) Doniphan, Edwards (both of these on the 1846 Expedition), Emory, Abert, etc., in the government reports; Dr. Coues's on "the Trail of a Spanish Pioneer"; Simpson's "Reconnaissance"; Black Mar's "Spanish Institutions of the Southwest".

And these are only a few of the indispensable English "Sources". The more I think about it, the more I am appalled at the idea of $50 to supply the University of New Mexico with a library on New Mexican history. My own little private library has $2000 worth of books on New Mexico--- and I wish I had more. I myself would not feel able to give a course on New Mexican history, unless besides the lectures, I could give my students access to at least $1000 worth of text books. Still, the most vital thing is for them to learn straight the things they do learn; and a smaller number of books, if they are the right books, can be vitalized by the right treatment.

I have some hope that by next year you can secure a critical edition of Benavides with facsimile and translations and notes. You should have the files of Out West in which many

The Southwest Society,
Archæological Institute of America

PRESIDENT, J. O. KOEPFLI
VICE-PRESIDENTS
GEN. H. G. OTIS   H. W. O'MELVENY   DR. NORMAN BRIDGE
TREASURER, W. C. PATTERSON   CURATOR, DR. F. M. PALMER   SECRETARY, CHAS. F. LUMMIS
EXECUTIVE COMMITTEE
CHARLES CASSATT DAVIS   JOSEPH SCOTT   MARY E. FOY
WM. H. BURNHAM   JOHN D. BICKNELL   J. A. FOSHAY
BURT ESTES HOWARD   J. A. MUNK   J. H. MARTINDALE
F. M. PALMER   CHAS. F. LUMMIS
JAMES SLAUSON

Los Angeles, Cal.

Prof. R.-3

original documents have been translated into English for the first time. There is also a good little series, cheap and popular, under the title of "The Trail Makers" published by Barnes & Co., New York, and including 'Cabeza de Vaca', 'Coronado' and De Soto. These, also, you will have to have.

I will be glad to give you any assistance in my power in this matter; for I love the old territory, which has been very good to me--- and am debtor everywhere to all scholars.

Sincerely yours,

Chas. F. Lummis –

Pardon my temporary secretary.

The Charles F. Lummis Book List

Bancroft, Hubert H. *History of Arizona and New Mexico*. Vol. III of *The Works of Hubert Howe Bancroft*. San Francisco: The History Company, 1889.

Prince, L. Bradford. *Historical Sketches of New Mexico*. Kansas City: Leggat Brothers, 1883.

Haines, Helen. *History of New Mexico from the Spanish Conquest to the Present Time, 1530-1890*. New York: New Mexico Historical Publ. Co., 1891.

Ladd, Horatio O. *The Story of New Mexico*. Boston: D. Lothrop Co., 1891.

Bandelier, Adolph F. *Historical Introduction to Studies Among the Sedentary Indians of New Mexico*. Vol. I; Boston: Papers of the Archeological Institute of America, 1883.

Bandelier, Adolph F. *Contributions to the History of the Southwestern Portion of the United States*. Vol. V; Boston: Papers of the Archeological Institute of America, 1890.

Bandelier, Adolph F. *Final Report of Investigations Among the Indians of the Southwestern United States, 1880 to 1885*. Vols. III and IV; Boston: Papers of the Archeological Institute of America, 1890-92.

Bandelier, Adolph F. *Report of an Archeological Tour into Mexico in the Year 1881*. Vol. II; Boston: Papers of the Archeological Institute of America, 1885.

Lummis, Charles F. *The Land of Poco Tiempo*. New York: Scribner's, 1893.

Lummis, Charles F. *The Spanish Pioneers*. Chicago, A.C. McClurg, 1893.

Kendall, George Wilkins. *Narrative of the Texan-Santa Fe Expedition*. New York: Harper & Brothers, 1844.

Gregg, Josiah. *Commerce of the Prairies*. 2 vols.; New York: Henry G. Langley, 1844.

Davis, William W.H. *El Gringo; or, New Mexico and Her People*. New York, Harper & Brothers, 1857.

Bartlett, John Russell. *Personal Narrative of Explorations and Incidents ... Connected with the United States and Mexican Boundary Commission*. 2 vols.; New York: D. Appleton & Company, 1854.

Hughes, John T. *Doniphan's Expedition; Conquest of New Mexico.* Cincinnati: J.A. and U.P. James, 1850.

Edwards, Frank S. *A Campaign in New Mexico with Colonel Doniphan.* Philadelphia: Carey and Hart, 1847.

Coues, Elliott (ed.). *On the Trail of a Spanish Pioneer: The Diary and Itinerary of Francisco Garcés in His Travels through Sonora, Arizona, and California, 1775-1776.* 2 vols.; New York: Francis P. Harper, 1900.

Simpson, James H. *Journal of a Military Reconnaissance from Santa Fe, New Mexico to the Navajo Country Made in 1849.* Philadelphia: Lippincott, Grambo and Company, 1852.

Blackmar, Frank W. *Spanish Institutions of the Southwest.* Baltimore: John Hopkins Press, 1891.

Death of a Son

Death of a Son: Amado Bandelier Lummis

One of the most shattering blows experienced by Charles F. Lummis was the death at age six of his eldest son Amado Bandelier Lummis. The child succumbed to pneumonia on Christmas Day 1900. At the time, Charles was editor of a regional magazine, *Out West*, published in Los Angeles. Each month's issue ran a column by the editor titled the "Lion's Den." Therein, the columnist habitually referred to himself as the Lion.

The January 1901 issue of *Out West* carried a brief, agonizing tribute in the Den to the Lion's lost cub.

OUT WEST
A MAGAZINE OF
THE OLD PACIFIC AND THE NEW
EDITED BY CHAS. F. LUMMIS

The Den is dim this month. It is at best but room for the Lion's passing thought; and today his thought paces up and down a narrow bound. He had just closed the eyes of one he hoped should one day do that office for him. He has just surrendered to the incorrupting flames the fair husk of what had been his tawnymaned cub; the lad he would have made a Man; the lad who *was* a Man at six — an old-fashioned, gentle, fearless little knight, whose first thought was always for others; whose last words, in the agony for breath, were "Yes, please;" a lad so big-eyed and slender and girlish-sweet that one half-thought Nature had mis-dressed him, until one noted that his undefiant eye never fell before any eye, nor ever wavered; that he never lied nor dodged, nor shirked his fault, nor skulked from its consequence... Love, we are born into; but to win respect is victory for a lifetime, long or short. It is well with the boy. But the Lion had not cubs to spare.

Charles Lummis' first son died of pneumona on Christmas Day, 1900, at age six.

5

The Death of Charles F. Lummis

The Death of Charles F. Lummis

This notice of the death of Charles Lummis was issued by the Associated Press on November 25, 1928:

Dr. Charles Fletcher Lummis, 69, author, explorer and historian, died at his home here today of cancer.

Last February physicians informed Dr. Lummis that he would not live more than a year.

With the knowledge that his days were numbered, Dr. Lummis worked at top speed to compile his life's poems and publish them before he died. This task was completed October 28, after which his strength slowly ebbed.

An advance copy of his *A Bronco Pegasus* reached Lummis from his publisher thirteen days late, but in time for him to hold a copy in his hand and listen to his own poems read to him as he lay dying.

A BRONCO PEGASUS

*Poems By
Charles F. Lummis*

www.ingramcontent.com/pod-product-compliance
Lightning Source LLC
Chambersburg PA
CBHW021014090426
42738CB00007B/783